Easy stitches and simple shapes set the stage for six summer tops that you'll enjoy making and wearing. Choose from a beautiful variety of neck lines, sleeve styles (including sleeveless), and yarn weights.

LEISURE ARTS, INC. • Maumelle, Arkansas

Lace-Trim V-NECK

EASY

SHOPPING LIST

Yarn (Light Weight) LIGHT 3

[2.6 ounces, 173 yards
(75 grams, 158 meters) per skein]:

- ☐ Main Color (Red) - {6-7-8}{9-10-11} skeins
- ☐ Contrasting Color (Grey) - 1 skein

Crochet Hooks

- ☐ Size H (5 mm)
- ☐ Size I (5.5 mm)

or sizes needed for gauge

Additional Supplies

- ☐ Yarn needle

SIZE INFORMATION

Size	Finished Chest Measurement	
Small	35"	(89 cm)
Medium	38¾"	(98.5 cm)
Large	43"	(109 cm)
1X	46¾"	(119 cm)
2X	51"	(129.5 cm)
3X	54¾"	(139 cm)

Size Note: We have printed the instructions for the sizes in different colors to make it easier for you to find:

- Size Small in Blue
- Size Medium in Pink
- Size Large in Green
- Size 1X in Brown
- Size 2X in Purple
- Size 3X in Orange

Instructions in Black apply to all sizes.

GAUGE INFORMATION

In pattern, with larger size hook,
18 sts and 17 rows = 4" (10 cm)

Gauge Swatch: 4¼" wide x 4" high (10.75 cm x 10 cm)

With Main Color and larger size hook, ch 20.

Rows 1-3: Work same as Back Body: 19 sts.

Rows 4-17: Repeat Rows 2 and 3, 7 times.

Finish off.

STITCH GUIDE

SINGLE CROCHET 2 TOGETHER
(abbreviated sc2tog)

Pull up a loop in each of next 2 sts, YO and draw through all 3 loops on hook **(counts as one sc)**.

BACK

BODY

With Main Color and larger size hook, ch {90-98-108}{116-126-134}.

Row 1 (Right side)**:** Sc in second ch from hook, (ch 1, skip next ch, sc in next ch) across: {44-48-53}{57-62-66} ch-1 sps.

Note: Loop a short piece of yarn around any stitch to mark Row 1 as **right** side.

Row 2: Ch 1, turn; sc in first sc and in next ch-1 sp, (ch 1, sc in next ch-1 sp) across, sc in last sc: {43-47-52}{56-61-65} ch-1 sps.

Row 3: Ch 1, turn; sc in first sc, ch 1, (sc in next ch-1 sp, ch 1) across, skip next sc, sc in last sc: {44-48-53}{57-62-66} ch-1 sps.

Rows 4-10: Repeat Rows 2 and 3, 3 times; then repeat Row 2 once **more**.

Each sc and ch-1 sp counts as one stitch.

Row 11 (Decrease row)**:** Ch 1, turn; beginning in first sc, sc2tog, sc in next ch-1 sp, (ch 1, sc in next ch-1 sp) across, sc2tog: {87-95-105}{113-123-131} sts.

Rows 12-22: Repeat Row 3, then repeat Rows 2 and 3, 5 times.

Row 23 (Decrease row)**:** Ch 1, turn; beginning in first sc, sc2tog, ch 1, (sc in next ch-1 sp, ch 1) across to last 3 sts, skip next sc, sc2tog: {85-93-103}{111-121-129} sts.

Maintaining pattern, decrease one stitch at each edge in same manner, every 12th row, 3 times **more**: {79-87-97}{105-115-123} sts.

Work even until Back measures approximately 16" (40.5 cm) from beginning ch, ending by working a **wrong** side row.

ARMHOLE SHAPING

Maintain established pattern throughout.

Row 1: Turn; slip st in first {8-10-13}{15-17-19} sts, ch 1, sc in next st, work across to last {8-10-13}{15-17-19} sts, leave remaining sts unworked: {63-67-71}{75-81-85} sts.

Rows 2 and 3: Ch 1, turn; beginning in first sc, sc2tog, work across to last 2 sts, sc2tog: {59-63-67}{71-77-81} sts.

Work even until Armholes measure approximately {6-6½-7}{7½-8-8½}"/ {15-16.5-18}{19-20.5-21.5} cm, ending by working a **wrong** side row.

RIGHT SHOULDER

Row 1: Ch 1, turn; work across first {15-17-19}{21-24-26} sts, leave remaining sts unworked.

Row 2: Ch 1, turn; beginning in first sc, sc2tog, work across: {14-16-18} {20-23-25} sts.

Rows 3-6: Ch 1, turn; work across.

Finish off.

LEFT SHOULDER

Row 1: With **right** side facing, skip next 29 sts from Right Shoulder and join Main Color with sc in next st ***(see Joining With Sc, page 30)***; work across: {15-17-19}{21-24-26} sts.

Row 2: Ch 1, turn; work across to last 2 sts, sc2tog: {14-16-18}{20-23-25} sts.

Rows 3-6: Ch 1, turn; work across.

Finish off.

FRONT

BODY

Work same as Back until Front measures approximately {14½-15-15½}{16-16-16}"/ {37-38-39.5}{40.5-40.5-40.5} cm from beginning ch, ending by working a **wrong** side row: {79-87-97} {105-115-123} sts.

ARMHOLE & LEFT NECK SHAPING

Maintain established pattern throughout.

SIZES SMALL, MEDIUM, & LARGE ONLY

Row 1: Ch 1, turn; work across first {39-43-48} sts, leave remaining sts unworked.

Decrease one stitch at neck edge, every row, {5-3-1} time(s): {34-40-47} sts.

Next Row: Turn; slip st in first {8-10-13} sts, ch 1, sc in next st, work across to last 2 sts, sc2tog: {25-29-33} sts.

Decrease one stitch at each edge, every row, twice: {21-25-29} sts.

Decrease one stitch at neck edge, every row, {5-7-9} times; then decrease every fourth row, twice: {14-16-18} sts.

SIZE 1X ONLY

Row 1: Turn; slip st in first 15 sts, ch 1, sc in next st, work across next 36 sts, leave remaining sts unworked: 37 sts.

Decrease one stitch at each edge, every row, twice: 33 sts.

Decrease one stitch at neck edge, every row, 11 times; then decrease every fourth row, twice: 20 sts.

SIZE 2X ONLY

Row 1: Turn; slip st in first 17 sts, ch 1, sc in next st, work across to last 17 sts, leave remaining sts unworked: 81 sts.

Row 2: Ch 1, turn; beginning in first sc, sc2tog, work across to last 2 sts, sc2tog: 79 sts.

Row 3: Ch 1, turn; beginning in first sc, sc2tog, work across next 37 sts, leave remaining sts unworked: 38 sts.

Decrease one stitch at neck edge, every row, 13 times; then decrease every fourth row, twice: 23 sts.

SIZE 3X ONLY

Row 1: Turn; slip st in first 19 sts, ch 1, sc in next st, work across to last 19 sts, leave remaining sts unworked: 85 sts.

Rows 2 and 3: Ch 1, turn; beginning in first sc, sc2tog, work across to last 2 sts, sc2tog: 81 sts.

Row 4: Ch 1, turn; work across.

Row 5: Ch 1, turn; work across first 40 sts, leave remaining sts unworked.

Decrease one stitch at neck edge, every row, 13 times; then decrease every fourth row, twice: 25 sts.

ALL SIZES

Work even until Armhole measures same as Back, ending by working a **wrong** side row.

Finish off leaving a long end for sewing.

ARMHOLE & RIGHT NECK SHAPING

SIZES SMALL, MEDIUM, & LARGE ONLY

Row 1: With **right** side facing, skip one st from Left Neck and join Main Color with sc in next st; work across: {39-43-48} sts.

Decrease one stitch at neck edge, every row, {5-3-1} times: {34-40-47} sts.

Next Row: Ch 1, turn; beginning in first sc, sc2tog, work across to last {8-10-13} sts, leave remaining sts unworked: {25-29-33} sts.

Work same as Left Neck Shaping.

SIZE 1X ONLY

Row 1: With **right** side facing, skip one st from Left Neck and join Main Color with sc in next st; work across to last 15 sts, leave remaining sts unworked: 37 sts.

Work same as Left Neck Shaping.

SIZE 2X ONLY

Row 1: With **right** side facing, skip one st from Left Neck and join Main Color with sc in next st; work across to last 2 sts, sc2tog: 38 sts.

Decrease one stitch at neck edge, every row, 13 times; then decrease every fourth row, twice: 23 sts.

SIZE 3X ONLY

Row 1: With **right** side facing, skip one st from Left Neck and join Main Color with sc in next st; work across: 40 sts.

Decrease one stitch at neck edge, every row, 13 times; then decrease every fourth row, twice: 25 sts.

ALL SIZES

Work even until Armhole measures same as Back, ending by working a **wrong** side row.

Finish off leaving a long end for sewing.

FINISHING

Whipstitch shoulder seams ***(Fig. 3a, page 30)***.

Whipstitch side seams ***(Fig. 3b, page 30)***.

ARMHOLE EDGING

Rnd 1: With **right** side facing and smaller size hook, join Main Color with sc at side seam; sc evenly around; join with slip st to first sc.

Rnd 2: Ch 1, working from **left** to **right**, work reverse sc in each sc around ***(Figs. 1a-d, page 30)***; join with slip st to first st, finish off.

NECK TRIM

With smaller size hook and Contrasting Color, ch 120.

Row 1 (Right side)**:** Sc in second ch from hook and in each ch across: 119 sc.

Note: Mark Row 1 as **right** side.

Row 2: Ch 4, turn; skip first 2 sc, dc in next sc, (ch 1, skip next sc, dc in next sc) across: 59 sps.

Row 3: Ch 1, turn; (sc, ch 1, sc) in each sp across, slip st in third ch of beginning ch 4; finish off leaving a long end for sewing.

Using photo, page 2, as a guide, place ends of Neck Trim together at center Front, with end of rows on one end across beginning chs at opposite end; sew Trim to neck edge.

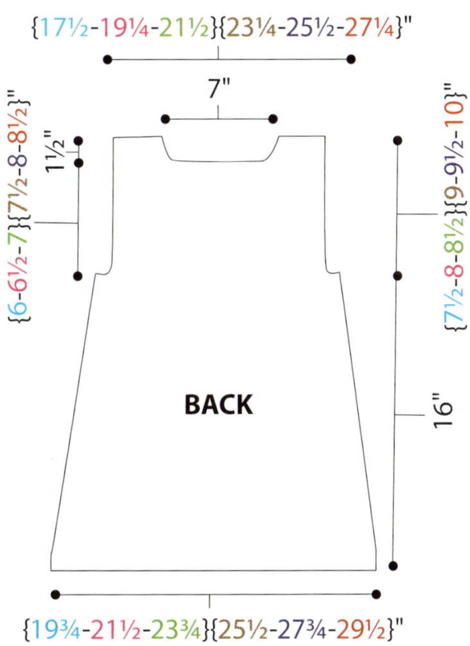

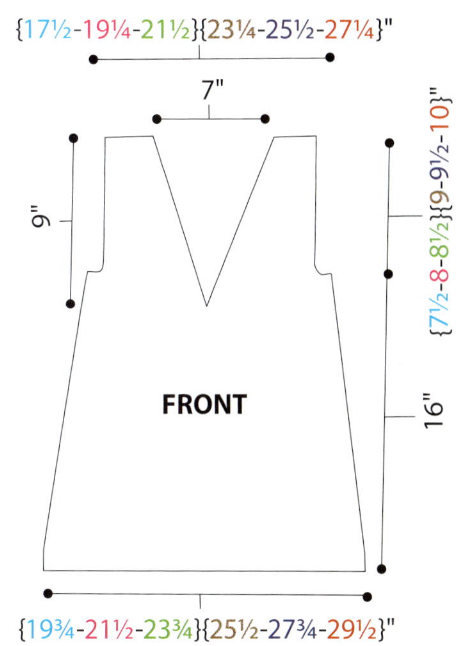

Enchanting EMPIRE

EASY

SHOPPING LIST

Yarn (Medium Weight) 4

[3.5 ounces, 186 yards
(100 grams, 170 meters) per skein]:

- ☐ Main Color (Gold) - {5-6-7}{8-9-10} skeins
- ☐ Contrasting Color (Ecru) - 1 skein

Crochet Hooks

- ☐ Size 7 (4.5 mm)
- ☐ Size H (5 mm)

or sizes needed for gauge

Additional Supplies

- ☐ Yarn needle

SIZE INFORMATION

Size	Finished Chest Measurement	
Small	35"	(89 cm)
Medium	38¾"	(98.5 cm)
Large	43"	(109 cm)
1X	46¾"	(119 cm)
2X	51"	(129.5 cm)
3X	54¾"	(139 cm)

Size Note: We have printed the instructions for the sizes in different colors to make it easier for you to find:

- Size Small in Blue
- Size Medium in Pink
- Size Large in Green
- Size 1X in Brown
- Size 2X in Purple
- Size 3X in Orange

Instructions in Black apply to all sizes.

GAUGE INFORMATION

In Bodice pattern, with smaller size hook,
18 sts and 17 rows = 4" (10 cm)

Gauge Swatch: 4¼" wide x 4" high (10.75 cm x 10 cm)

With Main Color and smaller size hook, ch 20.

Row 1 (Right side)**:** Sc in second ch from hook, (ch 1, skip next ch, sc in next ch) across: 19 sts.

Rows 2-17: Repeat Rows 3 and 4 of Back Bodice, page 8, 8 times.

Finish off.

STITCH GUIDE

SINGLE CROCHET 2 TOGETHER *(abbreviated sc2tog)*

Pull up a loop in each of next 2 sts, YO and draw through all 3 loops on hook (**counts as one sc**).

CLUSTER (uses one st)

★ YO, insert hook in st indicated, YO and pull up a loop, YO and draw through 2 loops on hook; repeat from ★ once **more**, YO and draw through all 3 loops on hook.

BACK

BODY

With Main Color and larger size hook, ch {82-92-102}{112-122-132}.

Row 1 (Right side)**:** Sc in second ch from hook, ★ ch 5, skip next 4 chs, sc in next ch; repeat from ★ across: {16-18-20}{22-24-26} ch-5 sps.

Note: Loop a short piece of yarn around any stitch to mark Row 1 as **right** side.

Row 2: Ch 3 (**counts as first dc**), turn; 2 dc in first sc, sc in next ch-5 sp, ★ (2 dc, ch 1, 2 dc) in next sc, sc in next ch-5 sp; repeat from ★ across to last sc, 3 dc in last sc: {15-17-19}{21-23-25} ch-1 sps.

Row 3: Ch 1, turn; sc in first dc, ★ ch 5, skip next 5 sts, sc in next ch-1 sp, ch 5; repeat from ★ across to last 6 sts, skip next 5 sts, sc in last dc: {16-18-20}{22-24-26} ch-5 sps.

Repeat Rows 2 and 3 for pattern until Body measures approximately {12½-13-13½}{13½-14-14½}"/{32-33-34.5}{34.5-35.5-37} cm from beginning ch, ending by working Row 2.

Next Row: Ch 1, turn; sc in first dc, ch 4, ★ skip next 5 sts, sc in next ch-1 sp, ch 4; repeat from ★ across to last 6 sts, skip next 5 sts, sc in last dc: {16-18-20}{22-24-26} ch-4 sps.

BODICE

SIZES SMALL, MEDIUM, & LARGE ONLY

Row 1: Using smaller size hook, ch 1, turn; sc in first sc, {3-2-2} sc in next ch-4 sp, sc in next sc, (4 sc in next ch-4 sp, sc in next sc) across to last ch-4 sp, {3-2-2} sc in last ch-4 sp, sc in last sc: {79-87-97} sc.

SIZES 1X, 2X, & 3X ONLY

Row 1: Using smaller size hook, ch 1, turn; sc in first sc, (3 sc in next ch-4 sp, sc in next sc) {3-3-4} times, (4 sc in next ch-4 sp, sc in next sc) across to last {3-3-4} ch-4 sps, (3 sc in next ch-4 sp, sc in next sc) across: {105-115-123} sc.

ALL SIZES

Row 2: Ch 1, turn; sc in first sc, (ch 1, skip next sc, sc in next sc) across: {39-43-48}{52-57-61} ch-1 sps.

Row 3: Ch 1, turn; sc in first sc and in next ch-1 sp, (ch 1, sc in next ch-1 sp) across, sc in last sc: {38-42-47}{51-56-60} ch-1 sps.

Row 4: Ch 1, turn; sc in first sc, ch 1, (sc in next ch-1 sp, ch 1) across, skip next sc, sc in last sc: {39-43-48}{52-57-61} ch-1 sps.

Repeat Rows 3 and 4 for pattern until Back measures approximately 17½" (44.5 cm) from beginning ch, ending by working a **wrong** side row.

ARMHOLE SHAPING

Each sc and ch-1 sp counts as one stitch. Maintain established pattern throughout.

Row 1: Turn; slip st in first {8-10-13}{15-17-19} sts, ch 1, sc in next st, work across to last {8-10-13}{15-17-19} sts, leave remaining sts unworked: {63-67-71}{75-81-85} sts.

SIZES SMALL & MEDIUM ONLY

Rows 2 and 3: Ch 1, turn; beginning in first sc, sc2tog, ch 1, (sc in next ch-1 sp, ch 1) across to last 3 sts, skip next sc, sc2tog: {59-63} sts.

SIZES LARGE, 1X, 2X, & 3X ONLY

Rows 2 and 3: Ch 1, turn; beginning in first sc, sc2tog, sc in next ch-1 sp, (ch 1, sc in next ch-1 sp) across, sc2tog: {67}{71-77-81} sts.

ALL SIZES

Work even until Armholes measure approximately {6½-7-7½}{8-8½-9}"/{16.5-18-19}{20.5-21.5-23} cm, ending by working a **wrong** side row.

RIGHT SHOULDER

Row 1: Ch 1, turn; work across first {15-17-19}{21-24-26} sts, leave remaining sts unworked.

Row 2: Ch 1, turn; beginning in first sc, sc2tog, work across: {14-16-18}{20-23-25} sts.

Rows 3-5: Ch 1, turn; work across.

Finish off.

LEFT SHOULDER

Row 1: With **right** side facing, skip next 29 sts from Right Shoulder and join Main Color with sc in next st ***(see Joining With Sc, page 30)***; work across: {15-17-19}{21-24-26} sts.

Row 2: Ch 1, turn; work across to last 2 sts, sc2tog: {14-16-18}{20-23-25} sts.

Rows 3-5: Ch 1, turn; work across.

Finish off.

FRONT

BODY

Work same as Back to Armhole Shaping: {39-43-48}{52-57-61} ch-1 sps.

ARMHOLE & LEFT NECK SHAPING

Maintain established pattern throughout.

Row 1: Turn; slip st in first {8-10-13}{15-17-19} sts, ch 1, sc in next st, work across {30-32-34}{36-39-41} sts, leave remaining sts unworked: {31-33-35}{37-40-42} sts.

Rows 2 and 3: Ch 1, turn; beginning in first sc, sc2tog, work across to last 2 sts, sc2tog: {27-29-31}{33-36-38} sts.

Continue to decrease one stitch at neck edge, every row, 2 times **more**; then decrease every other row, 11 times: {14-16-18}{20-23-25} sts.

Work even until Armhole measures same as Back.

Finish off leaving a long end for sewing.

ARMHOLE & RIGHT NECK SHAPING

Row 1: With **right** side facing, skip one st from Left Neck and join Main Color with sc in next st; work across to last {8-10-13}{15-17-19} sts, leave remaining sts unworked: {31-33-35}{37-40-42} sts.

Complete same as Armhole & Left Neck Shaping.

FINISHING

Whipstitch shoulder seams *(Fig. 3a, page 30)*.

Whipstitch side seams *(Fig. 3b, page 30)*, being careful to match rows.

NECK EDGING

Rnd 1: With **right** side facing and smaller size hook, join Main Color with sc at either shoulder seam; sc evenly around neck opening decreasing at center of Front; join with slip st to first sc.

Rnd 2: Ch 1, working from **left** to **right**, work reverse sc in each sc around *(Figs. 1a-d, page 30)*; join with slip st to first st, finish off.

ARMHOLE EDGING

Rnd 1: With **right** side facing and smaller size hook, join Main Color with sc at side seam; sc evenly around; join with slip st to first sc.

Rnd 2: Ch 1, working from **left** to **right**, work reverse sc in each sc around; join with slip st to first st, finish off.

BELT

With Contrasting Color and smaller size hook, ch 398.

Rnd 1: Slip st in second ch from hook, † ch 2, skip next 2 chs, work Cluster in next ch, ch 5, slip st in third ch from hook, ch 2, work Cluster in same ch, ch 2, skip next 2 chs, slip st in next ch †; repeat from † to † across, ch 1, slip st in same ch as last slip st; working in free loops of beginning ch *(Fig. 2, page 30)*, repeat from † to † across; finish off.

Sew the Belt across the Front at the beginning of the Bodice, making sure the ends of the Belt are the same length.

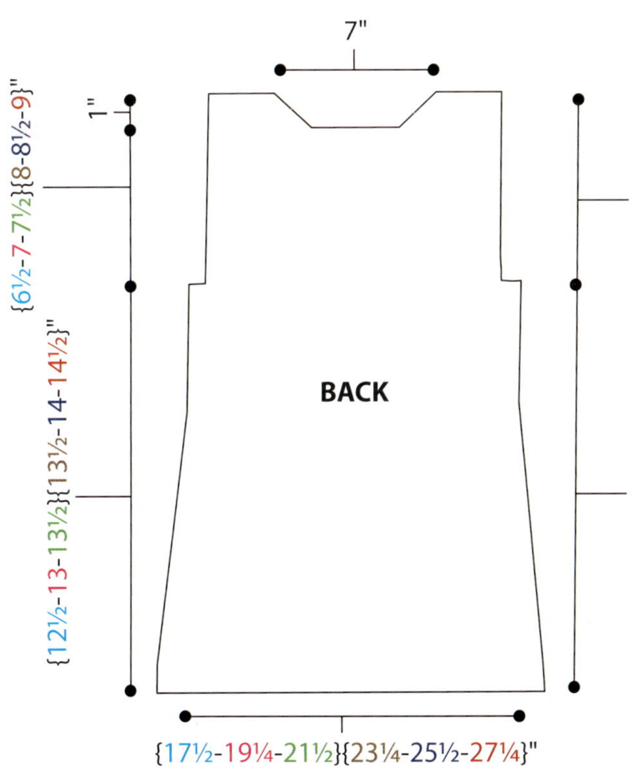

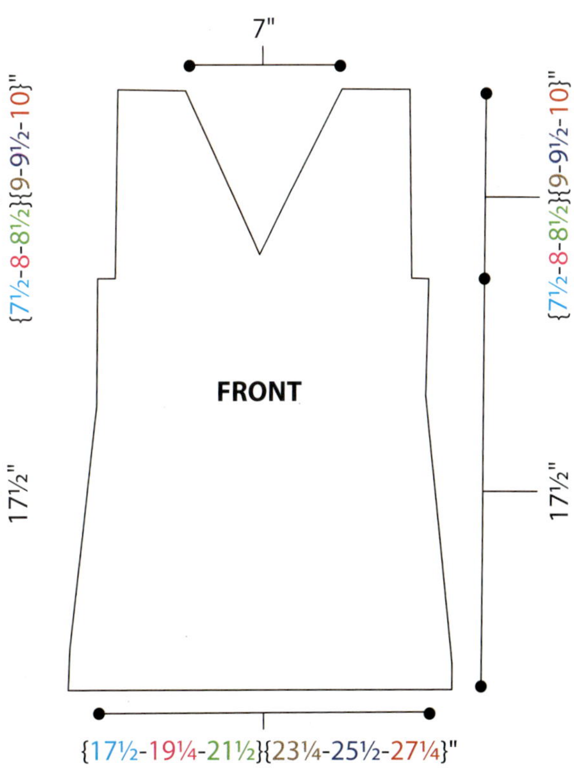

Ombre TEE

EASY

SHOPPING LIST

Yarn (Light Weight) 3

[1.75 ounces, 136 yards (50 grams, 125 meters) per skein]:

- ☐ Color A (Grey) - {7-8-9}{10-11-12} skeins
- ☐ Color B (Cream) - {5-6-7}{8-9-10} skeins
- ☐ Color C (Navy) - {5-5-6}{7-8-9} skeins

Crochet Hooks

- ☐ Size G (4 mm)
- ☐ Size H (5 mm)

or sizes needed for gauge

Additional Supplies

- ☐ Yarn needle

SIZE INFORMATION

Size	Finished Chest Measurement
Small	35½" (90 cm)
Medium	39½" (100.5 cm)
Large	43½" (110.5 cm)
1X	47½" (120.5 cm)
2X	51½" (131 cm)
3X	55½" (141 cm)

Size Note: We have printed the instructions for the sizes in different colors to make it easier for you to find:

- Size Small in Blue
- Size Medium in Pink
- Size Large in Green
- Size 1X in Brown
- Size 2X in Purple
- Size 3X in Orange

Instructions in Black apply to all sizes.

GAUGE INFORMATION

In pattern, with larger size hook and holding 2 strands of yarn together,
16 sts and 15 rows = 4" (10 cm)

Gauge Swatch: 4¼" wide x 4" high (10.75 cm x 10 cm)

With larger size hook and holding 2 strands of yarn together, ch 18.
Work same as Back Body for 15 rows: 17 sts.
Finish off.

STITCH GUIDE

SINGLE CROCHET 2 TOGETHER *(abbreviated sc2tog)*

Pull up a loop in each of next 2 sts, YO and draw through all 3 loops on hook **(counts as one sc)**.

CHANGING COLORS

Insert hook in last sc, YO and pull up a loop, drop strand(s) no longer neded, with strands indicated, YO and draw through both loops on hook ***(Fig. A)***. When changing only one of the strands, cut the extra strand.

Fig. A

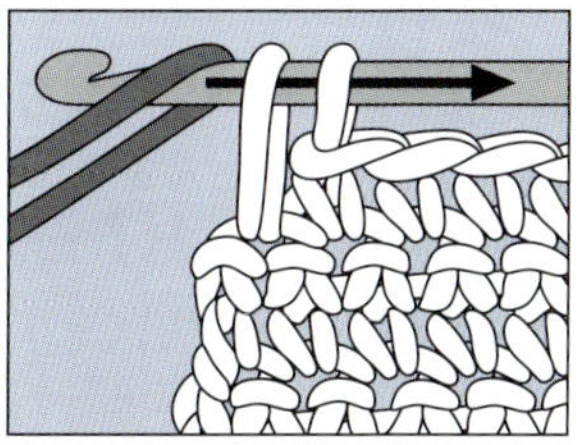

The pullover is worked holding two strands of yarn together throughout.

BACK

BODY

With larger size hook and holding 2 strands of Color C together, ch {72-80-88}{96-104-112}.

Row 1 (Right side)**:** Sc in second ch from hook, (ch 1, skip next ch, sc in next ch) across: {35-39-43}{47-51-55} ch 1 sps.

Note: Loop a short piece of yarn around any stitch to mark Row 1 as **right** side.

Row 2: Ch 1, turn; sc in first sc and in next ch-1 sp, (ch 1, sc in next ch-1 sp) across, sc in last sc: {34-38-42}{46-50-54} ch-1 sps.

Row 3: Ch 1, turn; sc in first sc, ch 1, (sc in next ch-1 sp, ch 1) across, skip next sc, sc in last sc: {35-39-43}{47-51-55} ch-1 sps.

Repeat Rows 2 and 3 for pattern until Body measures approximately 5" (12.5 cm) from beginning ch; at end of last row, change to one strand each of Color C and Color A.

Continue working in pattern for 5" (12.5 cm); at end of last row, change to two strands of Color A.

Continue working in pattern for 5" (12.5 cm); at end of last row, change to one strand each of Color A and Color B.

Continue working in pattern until Back measures approximately {17½-17-16½}{16-15½-15}"/{44.5-43-42}{40.5-39.5-38} cm from beginning ch, ending by working a **wrong** side row.

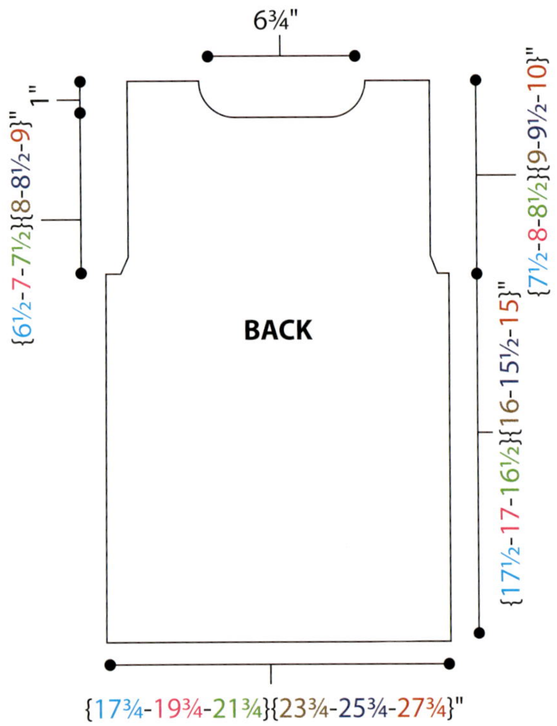

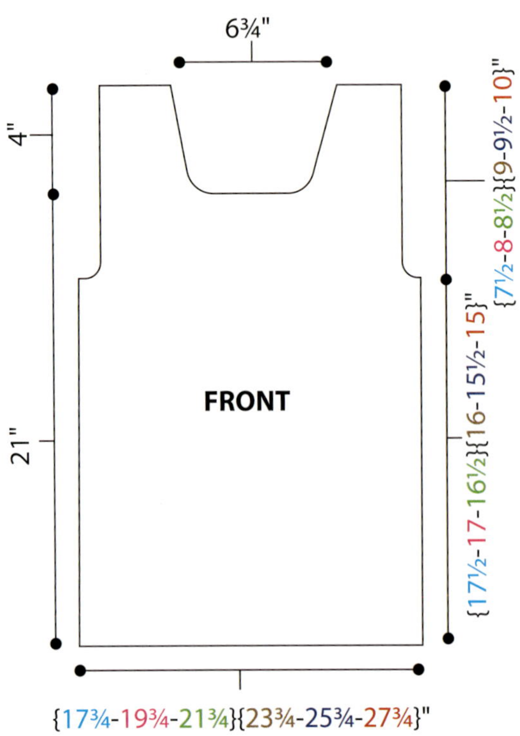

ARMHOLE SHAPING

Each sc and ch-1 sp counts as one stitch. Maintain established pattern throughout.

Row 1: Turn; slip st in first {4-6-7}{8-9-10} sts, ch 1, sc in next st, work across to last {4-6-7}{8-9-10} sts, leave remaining sts unworked: {63-67-73}{79-85-91} sts.

SIZES SMALL, MEDIUM, 1X, & 3X ONLY

Row 2 (Decrease row)**:** Ch 1, turn; beginning in first sc, sc2tog, ch 1, (sc in next ch-1 sp, ch 1) across to last 3 sts, skip next sc, sc2tog: {61-65}{77-89} sts.

SIZES LARGE & 2X ONLY

Row 2 (Decrease row)**:** Ch 1, turn; beginning in first sc, sc2tog, sc in next ch-1 sp, (ch 1, sc in next ch-1 sp) across, sc2tog: {71}{83} sts.

ALL SIZES

Decrease one stitch at each edge, every row, {0-0-1}{2-3-4} time(s) **more** ***(see Zeros, page 29)***; then decrease every other row, twice: {57-61-65}{69-73-77} sts.

Work even until color section measures 5" (12.5 cm); at end of last row, change to two strands of Color B.

Work even until Armholes measure approximately {6½-7-7½}{8-8½-9}"/{16.5-18-19}{20.5-21.5-23} cm, ending by working a **wrong** side row.

RIGHT SHOULDER

Row 1: Ch 1, turn; work across first {16-18-20}{22-24-26} sts, leave remaining sts unworked.

Row 2: Ch 1, turn; beginning in first sc, sc2tog, work across: {15-17-19}{21-23-25} sts.

Rows 3 and 4: Ch 1, turn; work across.

Finish off.

LEFT SHOULDER

Row 1: With **right** side facing, skip next 25 sts from Right Shoulder and join two strands of Color B with sc in next st *(see Joining With Sc, page 30)*; work across: {16-18-20}{22-24-26} sts.

Row 2: Ch 1, turn; work across to last 2 sts, sc2tog: {15-17-19}{21-23-25} sts.

Rows 3 and 4: Ch 1, turn; work across.

Finish off.

FRONT

BODY

Work same as Back until Front measures approximately 21" (53.5 cm) from beginning ch, ending by working a **wrong** side row: {57-61-65}{69-73-77} sts.

LEFT NECK SHAPING

Row 1: Ch 1, turn; work across first {19-21-23}{25-27-29} sts, leave remaining sts unworked.

Decrease one stitch at neck edge, every row, twice; then decrease every other row, twice: {15-17-19}{21-23-25} sts.

Work even until Armhole measures same as Back, ending by working a **wrong** side row.

Finish off leaving a long end for sewing.

RIGHT NECK SHAPING

Row 1: With **right** side facing, skip next 19 sts from Left Neck and join two strands of Color B with sc in next st; work across: {19-21-23}{25-27-29} sts.

Complete same as Left Neck Shaping: {15-17-19}{21-23-25} sts.

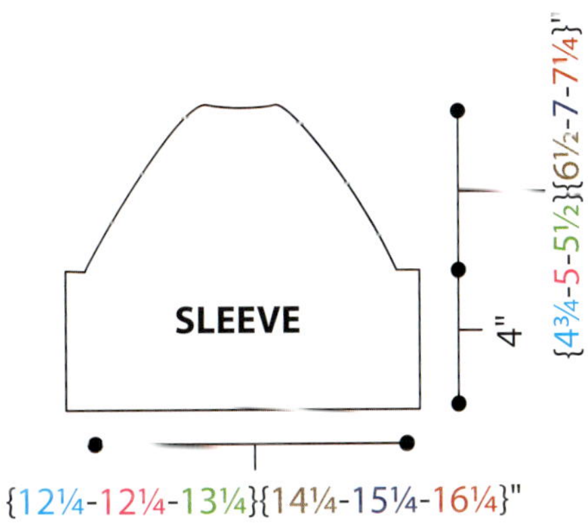

SLEEVE (Make 2)

BODY

With larger size hook and holding one strand each of Color A and Color B together, ch {50-50-54}{58-62-66}.

Work same as Back Body until Sleeve measures approximately 4" (10 cm) from beginning ch, ending by working a **wrong** side row: {49-49-53}{57-61-65} sts.

CAP SHAPING

Maintain established pattern throughout.

Row 1: Turn; slip st in first {4-6-7}{8-9-10} sts, ch 1, sc in next st, work across to last {4-6-7}{8-9-10} sts, leave remaining sts unworked: {41-37-39}{41-43-45} sts.

Work shaping as follows changing to 2 strands of Color B when Sleeve measures approximately {4½-5-5½}{6-6½-7}"/{11.5-12.5-14}{15-16.5-18} cm from beginning ch:

Decrease one stitch at each edge, every other row, {4-7-8}{10-11-11} times; then decrease every row, {8-3-3}{2-2-3} times: 17 sts.

Last Row: Turn; slip st in first 2 sts, ch 1, sc in next st, work across to last 2 sts, leave last 2 sts unworked; finish off.

FINISHING

Using one strand, whipstitch shoulder seams *(Fig. 3a, page 30)*.

Whipstitch Sleeves to Armhole *(Fig. 3b, page 30)*, matching stripes.

Whipstitch underarm and side in one continuous seam leaving last 3" (7.5 cm) on Front and Back unsewn.

NECK EDGING

Rnd 1: With **right** side facing, holding two strands of Color B together, and smaller size hook, join yarn with sc at either shoulder seam; sc evenly around neck opening; join with slip st to first sc.

Rnd 2: Ch 1, working from **left** to **right**, work reverse sc in each sc around *(Figs. 1a-d, page 30)*; join with slip st to first st, finish off.

Chic TANK

EASY

SHOPPING LIST

Yarn (Fine Weight) FINE 2

[1.75 ounces, 202 yards
(50 grams, 185 meters) per skein]:

- ☐ {5-6-7}{8-9-10} skeins

Crochet Hooks

- ☐ Size F (3.75 mm)
- ☐ Size G (4 mm)
  or sizes needed for gauge

Additional Supplies

- ☐ Yarn needle

SIZE INFORMATION

Size	Finished Chest Measurement	
Small	35"	(89 cm)
Medium	39¼"	(99.5 cm)
Large	43½"	(110.5 cm)
1X	47¾"	(121.5 cm)
2X	50½"	(128.5 cm)
3X	54½"	(138.5 cm)

Size Note: We have printed the instructions for the sizes in different colors to make it easier for you to find:

- Size Small in Blue
- Size Medium in Pink
- Size Large in Green
- Size 1X in Brown
- Size 2X in Purple
- Size 3X in Orange

Instructions in Black apply to all sizes.

GAUGE INFORMATION

In pattern, with larger size hook,
23 sts and 22 rows = 4" (10 cm)

Gauge Swatch: 4" (10 cm) square
With larger size hook, ch 24.

Rows 1-3: Work same as Back Body: 23 sts.

Rows 4-22: Repeat Rows 2 and 3, 9 times; then repeat Row 2 once **more**.

Finish off.

STITCH GUIDE

SINGLE CROCHET 2 TOGETHER
(abbreviated sc2tog)

Pull up a loop in each of next 2 sts, YO and draw through all 3 loops on hook **(counts as one sc)**.

BACK

BODY

With larger size hook, ch {102-114-126}{138-146-158}.

Row 1 (Right side)**:** Sc in second ch from hook, (ch 1, skip next ch, sc in next ch) across: {50-56-62}{68-72-78} ch-1 sps.

Note: Loop a short piece of yarn around any stitch to mark Row 1 as **right** side.

Row 2: Ch 1, turn; sc in first sc and in next ch-1 sp, (ch 1, sc in next ch-1 sp) across, sc in last sc: {49-55-61}{67-71-77} ch-1 sps.

Row 3: Ch 1, turn; sc in first sc, ch 1, (sc in next ch-1 sp, ch 1) across, skip next sc, sc in last sc: {50-56-62}{68-72-78} ch-1 sps.

Rows 4-10: Repeat Rows 2 and 3, 3 times; then repeat Row 2 once **more**.

Row 11: Ch 6 **(counts as first dc plus ch-3 sp, now and throughout)**, turn; skip first ch-1 sp, dc in next ch-1 sp, ch 3, ★ skip next ch-1 sp, dc in next ch-1 sp, ch 3; repeat from ★ across to last ch-1 sp, skip last ch-1 sp and next sc, dc in last sc: {26-29-32}{35-37-40} dc.

Row 12: Ch 1, turn; sc in first dc, (ch 3, sc in next dc) across.

Row 13: Ch 6, turn; dc in next sc, (ch 3, dc in next sc) across.

Row 14: Ch 1, turn; sc in first dc, ★ ch 1, skip next ch, sc in next ch, ch 1, skip next ch, sc in next dc; repeat from ★ across: {50-56-62}{68-72-78} ch-1 sps.

Rows 15-31: Repeat Rows 2 and 3, 8 times; then repeat Row 2 once **more**.

Rows 32-35: Repeat Rows 11-14.

Repeat Rows 2 and 3 for pattern until Back measures approximately {16½-16-15½}{15-14½-14}"/{42-40.5-39.5}{38-37-35.5} cm from beginning ch, ending by working a **wrong** side row.

ARMHOLE SHAPING

Each sc and ch-1 sp counts as one stitch. Maintain established pattern throughout.

Row 1: Turn; slip st in first {9-12-15}{19-20-23} sts, ch 1, sc in next st, work across to last {9-12-15}{19-20-23} sts, leave remaining sts unworked: {83-89-95}{99-105-111} sts.

SIZES SMALL, LARGE, 1X, & 3X ONLY

Rows 2 and 3 (Decrease rows)**:** Ch 1, turn; beginning in first sc, sc2tog, sc in next ch-1 sp, (ch 1, sc in next ch-1 sp) across, sc2tog: {79-91}{95-107} sts.

Row 4: Ch 1, turn; sc in first sc, ch 1, (sc in next ch-1 sp, ch 1) across, skip next sc, sc in last sc.

Row 5 (Decrease row)**:** Ch 1, turn; beginning in first sc, sc2tog, ch 1, (sc in next ch-1 sp, ch 1) across to last 3 sts, skip next sc, sc2tog: {77-89}{93-105} sts.

Row 6: Ch 1, turn; sc in first sc and in next ch-1 sp, (ch 1, sc in next ch-1 sp) across, sc in last sc.

Row 7 (Decrease row)**:** Ch 1, turn; beginning in first sc, sc2tog, sc in next ch-1 sp, (ch 1, sc in next ch-1 sp) across, sc2tog: {75-87}{91-103} sts.

SIZES MEDIUM & 2X ONLY

Rows 2 and 3 (Decrease rows)**:** Ch 1, turn; beginning in first sc, sc2tog, ch 1, (sc in next ch-1 sp, ch 1) across to last 3 sts, skip next sc, sc2tog: {85}{101} sts.

Row 4: Ch 1, turn; sc in first sc and in next ch-1 sp, (ch 1, sc in next ch-1 sp) across, sc in last sc.

Row 5 (Decrease row)**:** Ch 1, turn; beginning in first sc, sc2tog, sc in next ch-1 sp, (ch 1, sc in next ch-1 sp) across, sc2tog: {83}{99} sts.

Row 6: Ch 1, turn; sc in first sc, ch 1, (sc in next ch-1 sp, ch 1) across, skip next sc, sc in last sc.

Row 7 (Decrease row)**:** Ch 1, turn; beginning in first sc, sc2tog, ch 1, (sc in next ch-1 sp, ch 1) across to last 3 sts, skip next sc, sc2tog: {81}{97} sts.

ALL SIZES

Work even until Armholes measure approximately {6½-7-7½}{8-8½-9}"/{16.5-18-19}{20.5-21.5-23} cm, ending by working a **wrong** side row.

RIGHT SHOULDER

Row 1: Ch 1, turn; work across first {18-21-24}{26-29-32} sts, leave remaining sts unworked.

Row 2: Ch 1, turn; beginning in first sc, sc2tog, work across: {17-20-23}{25-28-31} sts.

Rows 3-6: Ch 1, turn; work across.

Finish off.

LEFT SHOULDER

Row 1: With **right** side facing, skip next 39 sts from Right Shoulder and join yarn with sc in next st ***(see Joining With Sc, page 30)***; work across: {18-21-24}{26-29-32} sts.

Row 2: Ch 1, turn; work across to last 2 sts, sc2tog: {17-20-23}{25-28-31} sts.

Rows 3-6: Ch 1, turn; work across.

Finish off.

FRONT

BODY

Work same as Back until Armholes measure approximately {1½-2-2½}{3-3½-4}"/{4-5-6.5}{7.5-9-10} cm, ending by working a **wrong** side row: {75-81-87}{91-97-103} sts.

LEFT NECK SHAPING

Row 1: Ch 1, turn; work across first {21-24-27}{29-32-35} sts, leave remaining sts unworked.

Decrease one stitch at neck edge, every row, twice; then decrease every other row, twice: {17-20-23}{25-28-31} sts.

Work even until Armhole measures same as Back, ending by working a **wrong** side row.

Finish off leaving a long end for sewing.

RIGHT NECK SHAPING

Row 1: With **right** side facing, skip next 33 sts from Left Neck and join yarn with sc in next st; work across: {21-24-27}{29-32-35} sts.

Complete same as Left Neck Shaping: {17-20-23}{25-28-31} sts.

FINISHING

Whipstitch shoulder seams ***(Fig. 3a, page 30)***.

Whipstitch side seams ***(Fig. 3b, page 30)***.

NECK EDGING

Rnd 1: With **right** side facing and smaller size hook, join yarn with sc at either shoulder seam; sc evenly around neck opening; join with slip st to first sc.

Rnd 2: Ch 1, working from **left** to **right**, work reverse sc in each sc around ***(Figs. 1a-d, page 30)***; join with slip st to first st, finish off.

ARMHOLE EDGING

Rnd 1: With **right** side facing and smaller size hook, join yarn with sc at side seam; sc evenly around; join with slip st to first sc.

Rnd 2: Ch 1, working from **left** to **right**, work reverse sc in each sc around; join with slip st to first st, finish off.

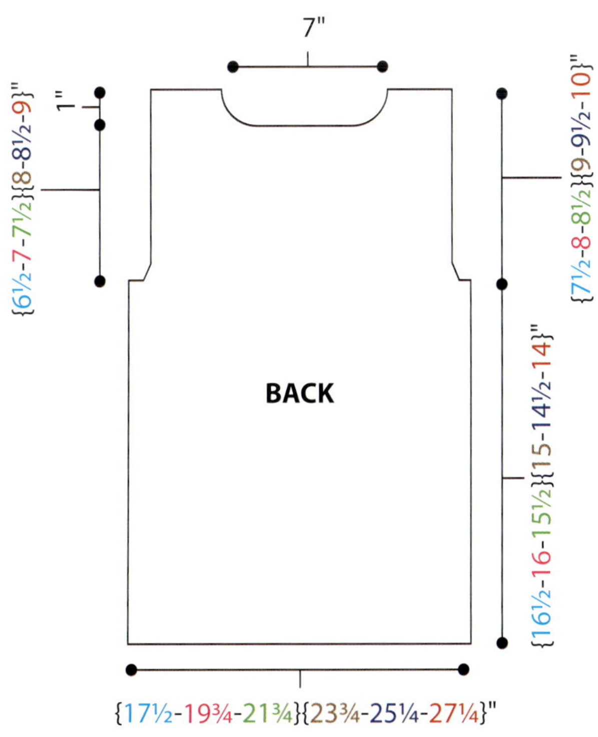

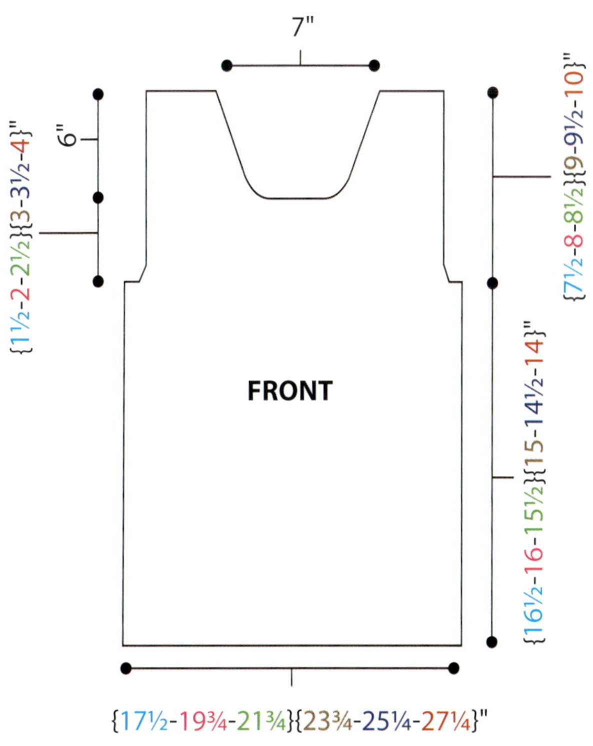

Belle TUNIC

EASY

SHOPPING LIST

Yarn (Light Weight)

[2.6 ounces, 173 yards (75 grams, 158 meters) per skein]:

☐ {10-11-12}{13-14-15} skeins

Crochet Hook

☐ Size I (5.5 mm)

or size needed for gauge

Additional Supplies

☐ Yarn needle

SIZE INFORMATION

Size	Finished Chest Measurement	
Small	35"	(89 cm)
Medium	38¾"	(98.5 cm)
Large	43"	(109 cm)
1X	46¾"	(119 cm)
2X	51"	(129.5 cm)
3X	54¾"	(139 cm)

Size Note: We have printed the instructions for the sizes in different colors to make it easier for you to find:

- Size Small in Blue
- Size Medium in Pink
- Size Large in Green
- Size 1X in Brown
- Size 2X in Purple
- Size 3X in Orange

Instructions in Black apply to all sizes.

GAUGE INFORMATION

In pattern,

18 sts and 17 rows = 4" (10 cm)

Gauge Swatch: 4¼" wide x 4" high (10.75 cm x 10 cm)

Ch 20.

Work same as Back Body for 17 rows: 19 sts.

Finish off.

STITCH GUIDE

SINGLE CROCHET 2 TOGETHER ***(abbreviated sc2tog)***

Pull up a loop in each of next 2 sts, YO and draw through all 3 loops on hook **(counts as one sc)**.

BACK

BODY

Ch {80-88-98}{106-116-124}.

Row 1 (Right side)**:** Sc in second ch from hook, (ch 1, skip next ch, sc in next ch) across: {39-43-48}{52-57-61} ch-1 sps.

Note: Loop a short piece of yarn around any stitch to mark Row 1 as **right** side.

Row 2: Ch 1, turn; sc in first sc and in next ch-1 sp, (ch 1, sc in next ch-1 sp) across, sc in last sc: {38-42-47}{51-56-60} ch-1 sps.

Row 3: Ch 1, turn; sc in first sc, ch 1, (sc in next ch-1 sp, ch 1) across, skip next sc, sc in last sc: {39-43-48}{52-57-61} ch-1 sps.

Repeat Rows 2 and 3 for pattern until Body measures approximately {16½-16-15½}{15-14½-14}"/{42-40.5-39.5}{38-37-35.5} cm from beginning ch, ending by working a **wrong** side row.

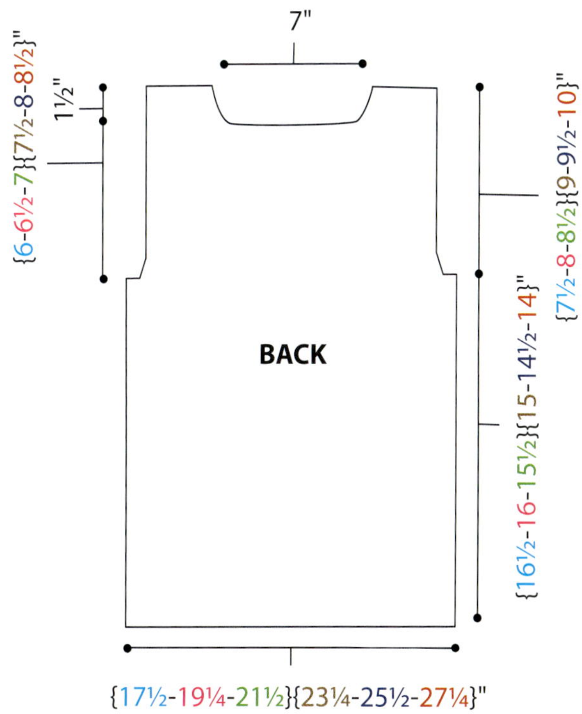

ARMHOLE SHAPING

Each sc and ch-1 sp counts as one stitch. Maintain established pattern throughout.

Row 1: Turn; slip st in first {5-6-7}{8-9-10} sts, ch 1, sc in next st, work across to last {5-6-7}{8-9-10} sts, leave remaining sts unworked: {69-75-83}{89-97-103} sts.

SIZES SMALL, LARGE, 1X, & 2X ONLY

Row 2 (Decrease row)**:** Ch 1, turn; beginning in first sc, sc2tog, sc in next ch-1 sp, (ch 1, sc in next ch-1 sp) across, sc2tog: {67-81}{87-95} sts.

SIZES MEDIUM & 3X ONLY

Row 2 (Decrease row)**:** Ch 1, turn; beginning in first sc, sc2tog, ch 1, (sc in next ch-1 sp, ch 1) across to last 3 sts, skip next sc, sc2tog: {73}{101} sts.

ALL SIZES

Decrease one stitch at each edge, every row, {2-3-5}{5-6-7} times **more**; then decrease every other row, {2-2-2}{3-3-3} times: {59-63-67}{71-77-81} sts.

Work even until Armholes measure approximately {6-6½-7}{7½-8-8½}"/{15-16.5-18}{19-20.5-21.5} cm, ending by working a **wrong** side row.

RIGHT SHOULDER

Row 1: Ch 1, turn; work across first {15-17-19}{21-24-26} sts, leave remaining sts unworked.

Row 2: Ch 1, turn; beginning in first sc, sc2tog, work across: {14-16-18}{20-23-25} sts.

Rows 3-6: Ch 1, turn; work across.

Finish off.

LEFT SHOULDER

Row 1: With **right** side facing, skip next 29 sts from Right Shoulder and join yarn with sc in next st *(see Joining With Sc, page 30)*; work across: {15-17-19}{21-24-26} sts.

Row 2: Ch 1, turn; work across to last 2 sts, sc2tog: {14-16-18}{20-23-25} sts.

Rows 3-6: Ch 1, turn; work across.

Finish off.

FRONT

Work same as Back through Row 2 of Armhole Shaping: {67-73-81}{87-95-101} sts.

Decrease one stitch at each edge, every row, {0-2-4}{5-6-7} times **more** *(see Zeros, page 29)*; then decrease every other row, {0-0-0}{0-1-1} time(s): {69-73}{77-81-85} sts.

Work even for {0-0-0}{1-0-1} row(s).

ARMHOLE & LEFT NECK SHAPING

SIZE SMALL ONLY

Row 1: Ch 1, turn; beginning in first sc, sc2tog, work across next 21 sts, leave remaining sts unworked: 22 sts.

Row 2: Ch 1, turn; beginning in first sc, sc2tog, work across to last 2 sts, sc2tog: 20 sts.

Row 3: Ch 1, turn; work across to last 2 sts, sc2tog: 19 sts.

Row 4: Ch 1, turn; beginning in first sc, sc2tog, work across to last 2 sts, sc2tog: 17 sts.

Row 5: Ch 1, turn; work across.

Rows 6 and 7: Repeat Rows 4 and 5: 15 sts.

Row 8: Ch 1, turn; beginning in first sc, sc2tog, work across: 14 sts.

SIZES MEDIUM, LARGE, & 1X ONLY

Row 1: Ch 1, turn; beginning in first sc, sc2tog, work across next {22-24}{26} sts, leave remaining sts unworked: {23-25}{27} sts.

Row 2: Ch 1, turn; beginning in first sc, sc2tog, work across: {22-24}{26} sts.

Row 3: Ch 1, turn; beginning in first sc, sc2tog, work across to last 2 sts, sc2tog: {20-22}{24} sts.

Rows 4-6: Ch 1, turn; beginning in first sc, sc2tog, work across: {17-19}{21} sts.

Row 7: Ch 1, turn; work across.

Row 8: Ch 1, turn; beginning in first sc, sc2tog, work across: {16-18} {20} sts.

SIZE 2X ONLY

Row 1: Ch 1, turn; work across first 30 sts, leave remaining sts unworked.

Row 2: Ch 1, turn; beginning in first sc, sc2tog, work across to last 2 sts, sc2tog: 28 sts.

Row 3: Ch 1, turn; work across to last 2 sts, sc2tog: 27 sts.

Row 4: Ch 1, turn; beginning in first sc, sc2tog, work across to last 2 sts, sc2tog: 25 sts.

Row 5: Ch 1, turn; work across.

Row 6: Ch 1, turn; beginning in first sc, sc2tog, work across: 24 sts.

Rows 7 and 8: Repeat Rows 5 and 6: 23 sts.

SIZE 3X ONLY

Row 1: Ch 1, turn; beginning in first sc, sc2tog, work across next 30 sts, leave remaining sts unworked: 31 sts.

Row 2: Ch 1, turn; beginning in first sc, sc2tog, work across: 30 sts.

Row 3: Ch 1, turn; beginning in first sc, sc2tog, work across to last 2 sts, sc2tog: 28 sts.

Row 4: Ch 1, turn; beginning in first sc, sc2tog, work across: 27 sts.

Row 5: Ch 1, turn; work across.

Rows 6-8: Repeat Rows 4 and 5 once, then repeat Row 4 once **more**: 25 sts.

ALL SIZES

Work even until Armhole measures same as Back, ending by working a **wrong** side row.

Finish off leaving a long end for sewing.

ARMHOLE & RIGHT NECK SHAPING

SIZE SMALL ONLY

Row 1: With **right** side facing, skip next 21 sts from Left Neck and join yarn with sc in next st; work across to last 2 sts, sc2tog: 22 sts.

Row 2: Ch 1, turn; beginning in first sc, sc2tog, work across to last 2 sts, sc2tog: 20 sts.

Row 3: Ch 1, turn; beginning in first sc, sc2tog, work across: 19 sts.

Row 4: Ch 1, turn; beginning in first sc, sc2tog, work across to last 2 sts, sc2tog: 17 sts.

Row 5: Ch 1, turn; work across.

Rows 6 and 7: Repeat Rows 4 and 5: 15 sts.

Row 8: Ch 1, turn; work across to last 2 sts, sc2tog: 14 sts.

SIZES MEDIUM, LARGE, & 1X ONLY

Row 1: With **right** side facing, skip next 21 sts from Left Neck and join yarn with sc in next st; work across to last 2 sts, sc2tog: {23-25}{27} sts.

Row 2: Ch 1, turn; work across to last 2 sts, sc2tog: {22-24}{26} sts.

Row 3: Ch 1, turn; beginning in first sc, sc2tog, work across to last 2 sts, sc2tog: {20-22}{24} sts.

Rows 4-6: Ch 1, turn; work across to last 2 sts, sc2tog: {17-19}{21} sts.

Row 7: Ch 1, turn; work across.

Row 8: Ch 1, turn; work across to last 2 sts, sc2tog: {16-18}{20} sts.

SIZE 2X ONLY

Row 1: With **right** side facing, skip next 21 sts from Left Neck and join yarn with sc in next st; work across: 30 sts.

Row 2: Ch 1, turn; beginning in first sc, sc2tog, work across to last 2 sts, sc2tog: 28 sts.

Row 3: Ch 1, turn; beginning in first sc, sc2tog, work across: 27 sts.

Row 4: Ch 1, turn; beginning in first sc, sc2tog, work across to last 2 sts, sc2tog: 25 sts.

Row 5: Ch 1, turn; work across.

Row 6: Ch 1, turn; work across to last 2 sts, sc2tog: 24 sts.

Rows 7 and 8: Repeat Rows 5 and 6: 23 sts.

SIZE 3X ONLY

Row 1: With **right** side facing, skip next 21 sts from Left Neck and join yarn with sc in next st; work across to last 2 sts, sc2tog: 31 sts.

Row 2: Ch 1, turn; work across to last 2 sts, sc2tog: 30 sts.

Row 3: Ch 1, turn; beginning in first sc, sc2tog, work across to last 2 sts, sc2tog: 28 sts.

Row 4: Ch 1, turn; work across to last 2 sts, sc2tog: 27 sts.

Row 5: Ch 1, turn; work across.

Rows 6-8: Repeat Rows 4 and 5 once, then repeat Row 4 once **more**: 25 sts.

ALL SIZES

Work even until Armhole measures same as Back, ending by working a **wrong** side row.

Finish off leaving a long end for sewing.

SLEEVE (Make 2)

BODY

Ch {68-72-76}{82-86-92}.

Work same as Back Body decreasing one stitch at each edge, every 14th row, 5 times: {57-61-65}{71-75-81} sts.

Work even until Sleeve measures approximately 17½" (44.5 cm) from beginning ch, ending by working a **wrong** side row.

CAP SHAPING

Maintain established pattern throughout.

Row 1: Turn; slip st in first {5-6-7}{8-9-10} sts, ch 1, sc in next st, work across to last {5-6-7}{8-9-10} sts, leave remaining sts unworked: {47-49-51}{55-57-61} sts.

Decrease one stitch at each edge, every other row, {7-8-9}{9-10-10} times; then decrease every row, {6-6-6}{8-8-10} times: 21 sts.

Next 2 Rows: Turn; slip st in first 2 sts, ch 1, sc in next st, work across to last 2 sts, leave last 2 sts unworked: 13 sts.

Finish off.

FINISHING

Whipstitch shoulder seams *(Fig. 3a, page 30)*.

Whipstitch Sleeves to Armhole *(Fig. 3b, page 30)*.

Whipstitch underarm and side in one continuous seam.

NECK EDGING

Rnd 1: With **right** side facing, join yarn with sc at either shoulder seam; sc evenly around neck opening; join with slip st to first sc.

Rnd 2: Ch 1, working from **left** to **right**, work reverse sc in each sc around *(Figs. 1a-d, page 30)*; join with slip st to first st, finish off.

SLEEVE TRIM

Rnd 1: With **right** side facing, working in sps and in free loops of beginning chs *(Fig. 2, page 30)*, join yarn with sc at seam; work {64-69-74}{79-84-89} sc evenly spaced around; join with slip st to first sc: {65-70-75}{80-85-90} sc.

Rnd 2: Ch 1, sc in same st as joining, ch 5, skip next 4 sc, ★ sc in next sc, ch 5, skip next 4 sc; repeat from ★ around; join with slip st to first sc.

Rnd 3: ★ 4 Sc in next ch-5 sp, (ch 3, slip st in third ch from hook) 3 times, 3 sc in same sp ch-5 sp; repeat from ★ around; join with slip st to first sc, finish off.

Repeat on second Sleeve.

BODY TRIM

Rnd 1: With **right** side facing, working in sps and in free loops of beginning chs, join yarn with sc at either seam; sc evenly around having a multiple of 5 sc; join with slip st to first sc.

Rnds 2 and 3: Work same as Sleeve Trim.

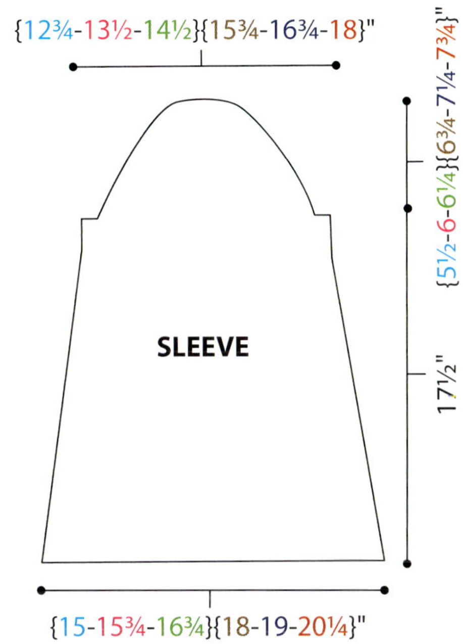

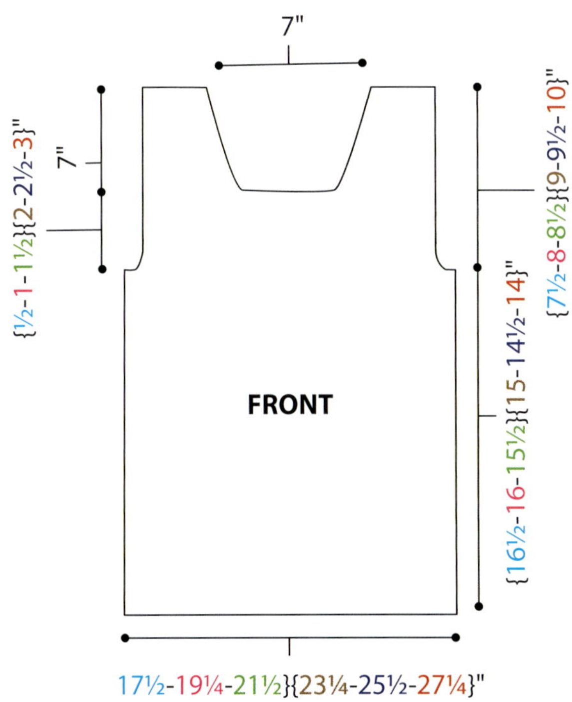

Sweet Boho TOP

EASY

SHOPPING LIST

Yarn (Medium Weight) MEDIUM 4

[3.5 ounces, 186 yards (100 grams, 170 meters) per skein]:

- ☐ Main Color (Mint) - {6-7-8}{9-10-11} skeins
- ☐ Contrasting Color (Ecru) - 1 skein

Crochet Hooks

- ☐ Size G (4 mm)
- ☐ Size 7 (4.5 mm)

or sizes needed for gauge

Additional Supplies

- ☐ Yarn needle

SIZE INFORMATION

Size	Finished Chest Measurement	
Small	35"	(89 cm)
Medium	38¾"	(98.5 cm)
Large	43"	(109 cm)
1X	46¾"	(119 cm)
2X	51"	(129.5 cm)
3X	54¾"	(139 cm)

Size Note: We have printed the instructions for the sizes in different colors to make it easier for you to find:

- Size Small in Blue
- Size Medium in Pink
- Size Large in Green
- Size 1X in Brown
- Size 2X in Purple
- Size 3X in Orange

Instructions in Black apply to all sizes.

GAUGE INFORMATION

In pattern, with larger size hook,
18 sts and 17 rows = 4" (10 cm)

Gauge Swatch: 4¼" wide x 4" high (10.75 cm x 10 cm)

With Main Color and larger size hook, ch 20.

Work same as Back Body for 17 rows: 19 sts.

Finish off.

STITCH GUIDE

SINGLE CROCHET 2 TOGETHER ***(abbreviated sc2tog)***

Pull up a loop in each of next 2 sts, YO and draw through all 3 loops on hook **(counts as one sc)**.

3 TR CLUSTER (uses one dc)

★ YO twice, insert hook in dc indicated, YO and pull up a loop, (YO and draw through 2 loops on hook) twice; repeat from ★ 2 times **more**, YO and draw through all 4 loops on hook.

BACK

BODY

With Main Color and larger size hook, ch {90-98-108}{116-126-134}.

Row 1 (Right side)**:** Sc in second ch from hook, (ch 1, skip next ch, sc in next ch) across: {44-48-53}{57-62-66} ch-1 sps.

Note: Loop a short piece of yarn around any stitch to mark Row 1 as **right** side.

Row 2: Ch 1, turn; sc in first sc and in next ch-1 sp, (ch 1, sc in next ch-1 sp) across, sc in last sc: {43-47-52}{56-61-65} ch-1 sps.

Row 3: Ch 1, turn; sc in first sc, ch 1, (sc in next ch-1 sp, ch 1) across, skip next sc, sc in last sc: {44-48-53}{57-62-66} ch-1 sps.

Rows 4-14: Repeat Rows 2 and 3, 5 times; then repeat Row 2 once **more**.

Each sc and ch-1 sp counts as one stitch.

Row 15 (Decrease row)**:** Ch 1, turn; beginning in first sc, sc2tog, sc in next ch-1 sp, (ch 1, sc in next ch-1 sp) across, sc2tog: {87-95-105}{113-123-131} sts.

Rows 16-28: Repeat Row 3, then repeat Rows 2 and 3, 6 times.

Row 29 (Decrease row)**:** Ch 1, turn; beginning in first sc, sc2tog, ch 1, (sc in next ch-1 sp, ch 1) across to last 3 sts, skip next sc, sc2tog: {85-93-103}{111-121-129} sts.

Maintaining pattern, decrease one stitch at each edge in same manner, every 16th row, 3 times: {79-87-97}{105-115-123} sts.

Work even until Back measures approximately 20½" (52 cm) from beginning ch, ending by working a **wrong** side row.

ARMHOLE SHAPING

Maintain established pattern throughout.

Row 1: Turn; slip st in first {8-10-13}{15-17-19} sts, ch 1, sc in next st, work across to last {8-10-13}{15-17-19} sts, leave remaining sts unworked: {63-67-71}{75-81-85} sts.

Rows 2 and 3: Ch 1, turn; beginning in first sc, sc2tog, work across to last 2 sts, sc2tog: {59-63-67}{71-77-81} sts.

Work even until Armholes measure approximately {6½-7-7½}{8-8½-9}"/{16.5-18-19}{20.5-21.5-23} cm, ending by working a **wrong** side row.

RIGHT SHOULDER

Row 1: Ch 1, turn; work across first {15-17-19}{21-24-26} sts, leave remaining sts unworked.

Row 2: Ch 1, turn; beginning in first sc, sc2tog, work across: {14-16-18}{20-23-25} sts.

Rows 3 and 4: Ch 1, turn; work across.

Finish off.

LEFT SHOULDER

Row 1: With **right** side facing, skip next 29 sts from Right Shoulder and join Main Color with sc in next st ***(see Joining With Sc, page 30)***; work across: {15-17-19}{21-24-26} sts.

Row 2: Ch 1, turn; work across to last 2 sts, sc2tog: {14-16-18}{20-23-25} sts.

Rows 3 and 4: Ch 1, turn; work across.

Finish off.

FRONT

BODY

With Main Color and larger size hook, ch {88-96-106}{114-124-132}.

Row 1 (Right side)**:** Sc in second ch from hook, (ch 1, skip next ch, sc in next ch) across: {43-47-52}{56-61-65} ch-1 sps.

Note: Mark Row 1 as **right** side.

Row 2: Ch 1, turn; sc in first sc and in next ch-1 sp, (ch 1, sc in next ch-1 sp) across, sc in last sc: {42-46-51}{55-60-64} ch-1 sps.

Row 3: Ch 1, turn; sc in first sc, ch 1, (sc in next ch-1 sp, ch 1) across, skip next sc, sc in last sc: {43-47-52}{56-61-65} ch-1 sps.

Repeat Rows 2 and 3 for pattern decreasing one stitch at each edge on Row 15; then decrease every 14th row, once; then decrease every 16th row, twice: {79-87-97}{105-115-123} sts.

Work even until Front measures approximately {16-16½-16½}{16½-16½-16½}"/{40.5-42-42}{42-42-42} cm from beginning ch, ending by working a **wrong** side row.

ARMHOLE & LEFT PLACKET SHAPING

Maintain established pattern throughout.

SIZE SMALL ONLY

Row 1: Ch 1, turn; work across 28 sts, leave remaining sts unworked.

Row 2: Ch 1, turn; work across.

Row 3: Turn; slip st in first 8 sts, ch 1, sc in next st, work across: 20 sts.

Decrease one stitch at Armhole edge, every row, twice: 18 sts.

SIZE MEDIUM ONLY

Row 1: Turn; slip st in first 10 sts, ch 1, sc in next st, work across next 21 sts, leave remaining sts unworked: 22 sts.

Decrease one stitch at Armhole edge, every row, twice: 20 sts.

SIZE LARGE ONLY

Row 1: Turn; slip st in first 13 sts, ch 1, sc in next st, work across to last 13 sts, leave remaining sts unworked: 71 sts.

Row 2: Ch 1, turn; beginning in first sc, sc2tog, work across to last 2 sts, sc2tog: 69 sts.

Row 3: Ch 1, turn; beginning in first sc, sc2tog, work across 21 sts, leave remaining sts unworked: 22 sts.

SIZES 1X, 2X, & 3X ONLY

Row 1: Turn; slip st in first {15-17-19} sts, ch 1, sc in next st, work across to last {15-17-19} sts, leave remaining sts unworked: {75-81-85} sts.

Rows 2 and 3: Ch 1, turn; beginning in first sc, sc2tog, work across to last 2 sts, sc2tog: {71-77-81} sts.

Work even for {1-3-5} row(s).

Next Row: Ch 1, turn; work across {24-27-29} sts, leave remaining sts unworked.

ALL SIZES

Work even until Left Front neck edge measures approximately 5" (12.5 cm).

NECK SHAPING

Decrease one stitch at neck edge, every row, twice; then decrease every other row, twice: {14-16-18} {20-23-25} sts.

Work even until Armhole measures same as Back, ending by working a **wrong** side row.

Finish off leaving a long end for sewing.

ARMHOLE & RIGHT PLACKET SHAPING

SIZE SMALL ONLY

Row 1: With **right** side facing, skip next 23 sts from Left Front and join Main Color with sc in next st; work across: 28 sts.

Row 2: Ch 1, turn; work across.

Row 3: Ch 1, turn; work across to last 8 sts, leave remaining sts unworked: 20 sts.

Decrease one stitch at Armhole edge, every row, twice: 18 sts.

SIZE MEDIUM ONLY

Row 1: With **right** side facing, skip next 23 sts from Left Placket and join Main Color with sc in next st; work across to last 10 sts, leave remaining sts unworked: 22 sts.

Decrease one stitch at Armhole edge, every row, twice: 20 sts.

SIZE LARGE ONLY

Row 1: With **right** side facing, skip next 23 sts from Left Placket and join Main Color with sc in next st; work across to last 2 sts, sc2tog: 22 sts.

SIZES 1X, 2X, & 3X ONLY

Row 1: With **right** side facing, skip next 23 sts from Left Placket and join Main Color with sc in next st; work across: {24-27-29} sts.

ALL SIZES

Work even until Right Front Placket measures approximately 5" (12.5 cm).

NECK SHAPING

Work same as Left Neck Shaping.

PLACKET EDGING (Make 2)

With Contrasting Color and smaller size hook, ch 28.

Row 1 (Right side)**:** Dc in sixth ch from hook **(5 skipped chs count as first dc plus ch-1 sp)**, (ch 1, skip next ch, dc in next ch) across: 12 ch-1 sps.

Note: Mark Row 1 as **right** side.

Rows 2-4: Ch 4 **(counts as first dc plus ch-1 sp)**, turn; dc in next dc, (ch 1, dc in next dc) across: 13 dc.

Row 5: Ch 1, turn; sc in first dc, ★ ch 3, work 3-tr Cluster in next dc, ch 3, sc in next dc; repeat from ★ across; finish off.

Using photo as a guide for placement, whipstitch long edge of Placket Edgings to end of rows of Front opening, between skipped sts and Neck Shaping ***(Figs. 3a & b, page 30)***, then whipstitch end of rows of Placket Edgings to skipped sts on Body, leaving a space between the Edgings.

FINISHING

Whipstitch shoulder seams.

Whipstitch side seams, beginning at armhole and leaving last 2" (5 cm) on Front and last 6" (15 cm) on Back unsewn.

NECK EDGING

Row 1: With **right** side facing and smaller size hook, join Main Color with sc at beginning of Right Neck Shaping; sc evenly across neck opening.

Row 2: Ch 1, do **not** turn; working from **left** to **right**, work reverse sc in each sc across ***(Figs. 1a-d, page 30)***; finish off.

ARMHOLE EDGING

Rnd 1: With **right** side facing and smaller size hook, join Main Color with sc at side seam; sc evenly around; join with slip st to first sc.

Rnd 2: Ch 1, working from **left** to **right**, work reverse sc in each sc around; join with slip st to first st, finish off.

TIE (Make 2)

Cut 3 lengths of Contrasting Color, approximately 48" (122 cm) long.

Holding all 3 strands together, tie the ends together to form a circle. Loop the circle over a door handle, and insert a pencil into the loop.

Pull tightly and twist the yarn by spinning the pencil clockwise until tight. Keeping the pencil end taut, place a finger halfway across the length of twisted yarn, and fold the yarn in half, matching the pencil end with the loop over the door handle. Remove your finger, letting the yarn twist on itself.

Tie overhand knots to secure the ends leaving 1" (2.5 cm) free for tassel. Cut the loops and trim the ends.

Sew a Tie to corner of each Placket Edging.

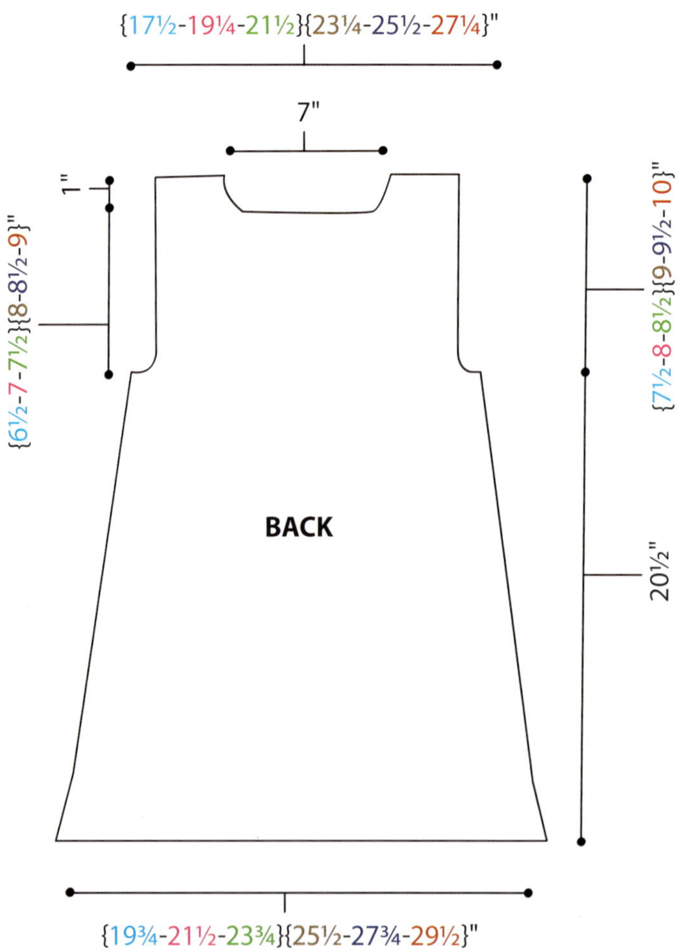

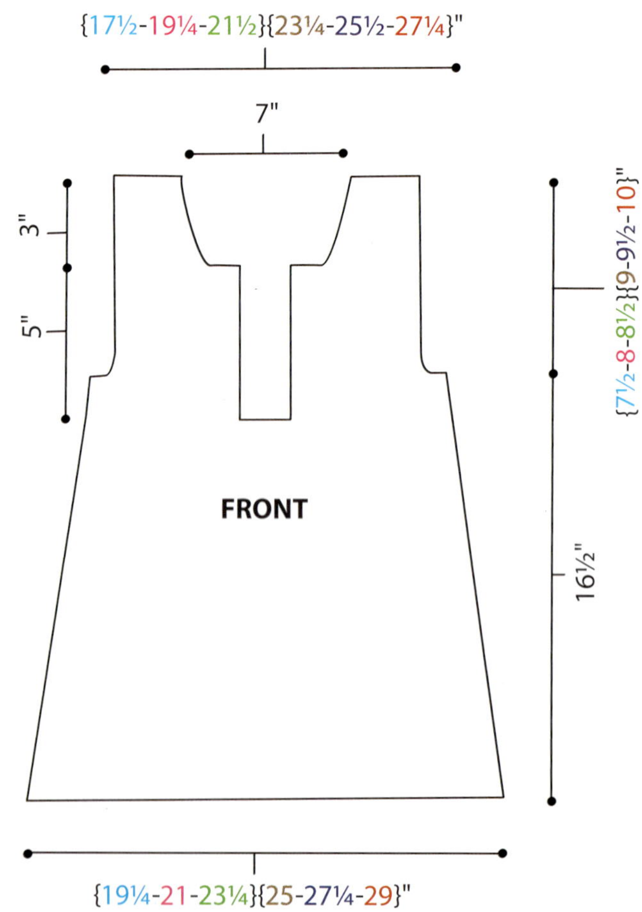

GENERAL INSTRUCTIONS

ABBREVIATIONS

ch(s)	chain(s)
cm	centimeters
dc	double crochet(s)
mm	millimeters
Rnd(s)	Round(s)
sc	single crochet(s)
sc2tog	single crochet 2 together
sp(s)	space(s)
st(s)	stitch(es)
tr	treble crochet(s)
YO	yarn over

CROCHET HOOKS	
U.S.	**Metric mm**
B-1	2.25
C-2	2.75
D-3	3.25
E-4	3.5
F-5	3.75
G-6	4
7	4.5
H-8	5
I-9	5.5
J-10	6
K-10½	6.5
L-11	8
M/N-13	9
N/P-15	10
P/Q	15
Q	16
S	19

SYMBOLS & TERMS

★ — work instructions following ★ as many **more** times as indicated in addition to the first time.

† to † — work all instructions from first † to second † **as many** times as specified.

( ) or **[ ]** — work enclosed instructions **as many** times as specified by the number immediately following **or** work all enclosed instructions in the stitch or space indicated **or** contains explanatory remarks.

colon (:) — the number(s) given after a colon at the end of a row or round denote(s) the number of stitches or spaces you should have on that row or round.

work even — work without increasing or decreasing in the established pattern.

GAUGE

Exact gauge is essential for proper fit. Before beginning your project, make the sample swatch given in the individual instructions in the yarn and hook specified. After completing the swatch, measure it, counting your stitches and rows carefully. If your swatch is larger or smaller than specified, **make another, changing hook size to get the correct gauge**. Keep trying until you find the size hook that will give you the specified gauge.

ZEROS

To consolidate the length of an involved pattern, zeros are sometimes used so that all sizes can be combined. For example, decrease one stitch at each edge, {0-0-1} time(s) means the first two sizes would do nothing and the last size would decrease once.

Yarn Weight Symbol & Names	LACE 0	SUPER FINE 1	FINE 2	LIGHT 3	MEDIUM 4	BULKY 5	SUPER BULKY 6	JUMBO 7
Type of Yarns in Category	Fingering, size 10 crochet thread	Sock, Fingering, Baby	Sport, Baby	DK, Light Worsted	Worsted, Afghan, Aran	Chunky, Craft, Rug	Super Bulky, Roving	Jumbo, Roving
Crochet Gauge* Ranges in Single Crochet to 4" (10 cm)	32-42 sts**	21-32 sts	16-20 sts	12-17 sts	11-14 sts	8-11 sts	6-9 sts	5 sts and fewer
Advised Hook Size Range	Steel*** 6 to 8, Regular hook B-1	B-1 to E-4	E-4 to 7	7 to I-9	I-9 to K-10½	K-10½ to M/N-13	M/N-13 to Q	Q and larger

*GUIDELINES ONLY: The chart above reflects the most commonly used gauges and hook sizes for specific yarn categories.

JOINING WITH SC

When instructed to join with sc, begin with a slip knot on hook. Insert hook in stitch or space indicated, YO and pull up a loop, YO and draw through both loops on hook.

REVERSE SINGLE CROCHET *(abbreviated reverse sc)*

Working from **left** to **right**, insert hook in st to right of hook ***(Fig. 1a)***, YO and draw through, under and to left of loop on hook (2 loops on hook) ***(Fig. 1b)***, YO and draw through both loops on hook ***(Figs. 1c & d)***.

Fig. 1a

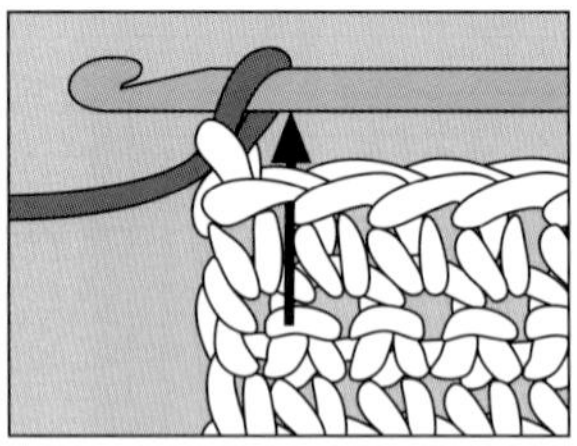

Fig. 1b

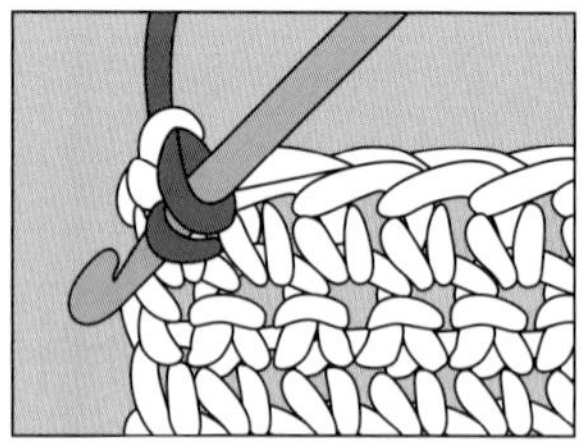

Fig. 1c

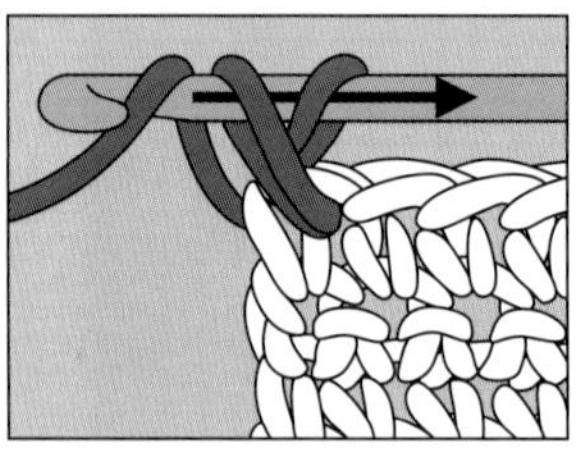

Fig. 1d

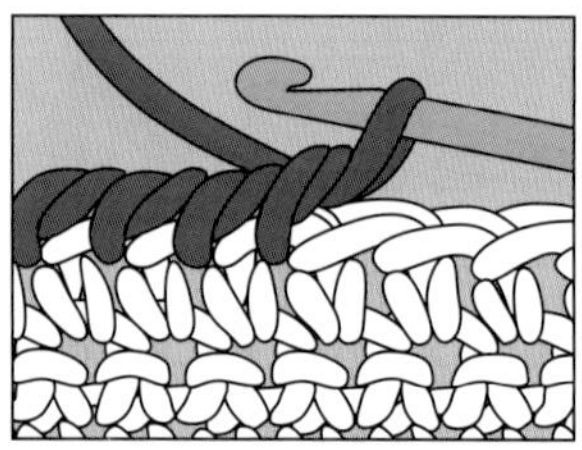

FREE LOOPS OF A CHAIN

When instructed to work in free loops of a chain, work in loop indicated by arrow ***(Fig. 2)***.

Fig. 2

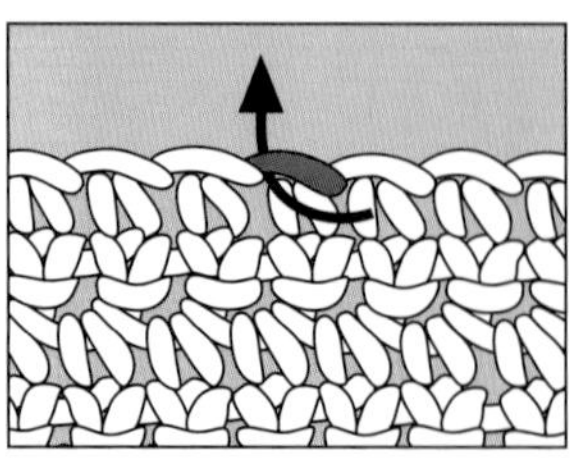

WHIPSTITCH

With **wrong** sides together, sew through both pieces once to secure the beginning of the seam, leaving an ample yarn end to weave in later. Insert the needle from **right** to **left** through two strands on each stitch of each piece ***(Fig. 3a)*** **or** through ends of rows ***(Fig. 3b)***. Bring the needle around and insert it from **right** to **left** through the next strands on both pieces.

Repeat along the edge, being careful to match stitches and rows.

Fig. 3a

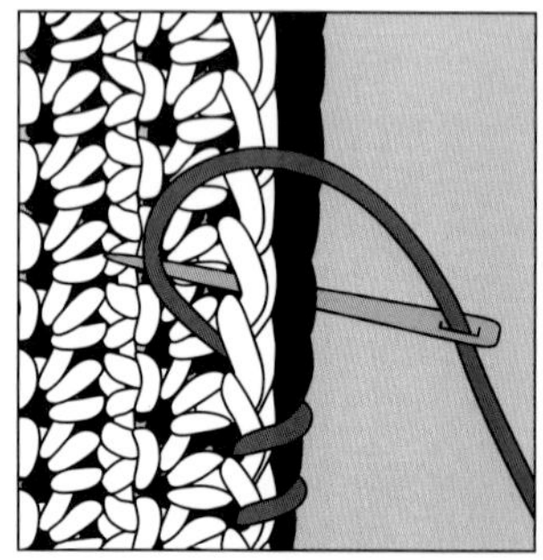

Fig. 3b

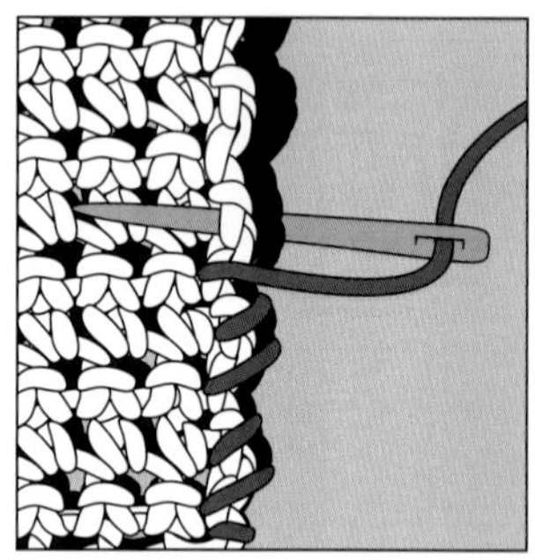

CROCHET TERMINOLOGY

UNITED STATES		INTERNATIONAL
slip stitch (slip st)	=	single crochet (sc)
single crochet (sc)	=	double crochet (dc)
half double crochet (hdc)	=	half treble crochet (htr)
double crochet (dc)	=	treble crochet (tr)
treble crochet (tr)	=	double treble crochet (dtr)
double treble crochet (dtr)	=	triple treble crochet (ttr)
triple treble crochet (tr tr)	=	quadruple treble crochet (qtr)
skip	=	miss

BEGINNER	Projects for first-time crocheters using basic stitches. Minimal shaping.
EASY	Projects using yarn with basic stitches, repetitive stitch patterns, simple color changes, and simple shaping and finishing.
INTERMEDIATE	Projects using a variety of techniques, such as basic lace patterns or color patterns, mid-level shaping and finishing.
EXPERIENCED	Projects with intricate stitch patterns, techniques and dimension, such as non-repeating patterns, multi-color techniques, fine threads, small hooks, detailed shaping and refined finishing.

MEET MELISSA LEAPMAN

With more than 800 knit and crochet designs in print, Melissa Leapman is one of the most widely published American designers working today.

She began her design career by freelancing for leading ready-to-wear design houses in New York City. She also created designs to help top yarn companies promote their new and existing yarns each season. Her ability to quickly develop fully envisioned garments put her skills in great demand.

Through the years, Leisure Arts has published more than 40 books of Melissa's fabulous designs. Melissa is also the host of several Leisure Arts DVDs in the best-selling teach-yourself series, "I Can't Believe I'm Knitting" and "I Can't Believe I'm Crocheting."

Nationally, her designs have been featured in numerous magazines, and her workshops on knitting and crochet are consistently popular with crafters of all skill levels. She has taught at major events such as STITCHES, Vogue Knitting LIVE, and The Knitting Guild Association conferences, as well as at hundreds of yarn shops and local guild events across the country.

To find more of Melissa's designs, visit LeisureArts.com, Melissa's Facebook page, and Ravelry.com.

YARN INFORMATION

The tops in this book were made using a variety of yarn weights. Any brand of the specific weight of yarn may be used. It is best to refer to the yardage/meters when determining how many balls or skeins to purchase. Remember, in order for your item to be the correct size, it is not the brand of yarn that matters, but the GAUGE/TENSION that is important.

For your convenience, listed below are the yarns used to create our photography models. Because yarn manufacturers make frequent changes in their product lines, you may sometimes find it necessary to use a substitute yarn or to search for the discontinued product at alternate suppliers (locally or online).

LACE-TRIM V-NECK

Lion Brand® Modern Baby®
Main Color - #113 Red
Contrasting Color - #149 Grey

ENCHANTING EMPIRE

Lion Brand® 24/7 Cotton®
Main Color - #158 Goldenrod
Contrasting Color - #098 Ecru

OMBRE TEE

Patons® Grace™
Color A - #62044 Clay
Color B - #62008 Natural
Color C - #62110 Navy

CHIC TANK

Lion Brand® Vanna's Glamour®
#149 Moonstone

BELLE TUNIC

Lion Brand® Modern Baby®
#098 Cream

SWEET BOHO TOP

Lion Brand® 24/7 Cotton®
Main Color - #156 Mint
Contrasting Color - #098 Ecru

We have made every effort to ensure that these instructions are accurate and complete.
We cannot, however, be responsible for human error, typographical mistakes, or variations in individual work.

Production Team: Instructional/Technical Editor - Cathy Hardy; Editorial Writer - Susan Frantz Wiles; Graphic Artist - Kellie McAnulty; Senior Graphic Artist - Lora Puls; Photo Stylist - Lori Wenger; and Photographer - Jason Masters.